GRADE

5

The Syllabus of Examinations should be read for details of requirements, especially those for scales, aural tests and sight-reading. Attention should be paid to the Special Notices on the inside front cover, where warning is given of any changes.

The syllabus is obtainable from music retailers or from The Associated Board of the Royal Schools of Music, 24 Portland Place, London W1B 1LU (please send a stamped addressed C5 (162mm × 229mm) envelope).

In examination centres outside the UK, information and syllabuses may be obtained from the Local Representative.

This book is to be returned on or before the last date stamped below

CONTENTS

Where appropriate, pieces in this volume have been checked with original source material and edited as necessary for instructional purposes. Fingering, phrasing, bowing, metronome marks and the editorial realization of ornaments (where given) are for guidance but are not comprehensive or obligatory.

DO NOT
PHOTOCOPY
© MUSIC

Alternative pieces for this grade

D1081385

© 2000 by The Associated Board of the Royal Schools of Music

No part of this publication may be copied or reproduced in any form or by any means without the prior permission of the publishers.

Music origination by Jack Thompson.
Cover by Økvik Design.
Printed in England by Halstan & Co. Ltd, Amersham, Bucks.

Allegro con spirito

First movement from Sonata in D, Op. 16 No. 5

DO NOT
PHOTOCOPY
© MUSIC

Edited by
Richard Jones

J. C. BACH

Johann Christian Bach (1735–82) was the famous Johann Sebastian's youngest son. This sonata is one of 33 written for piano or harpsichord 'with an accompaniment' for violin. Although the piano has the lion's share of the semiquavers, the violin holds its own in the musical conversation. Crossed slurs and bracketed dynamics and articulation marks (piano) are editorial suggestions only.

© 2000 by The Associated Board of the Royal Schools of Music

Allegro

Second movement from Sonata in F, Op. 1 No. 12, HWV 370

DO NOT PHOTOCOPY © MUSIC

Edited by
Richard Jones

Attributed to HANDEL

In 1732 Handel's publisher John Walsh produced a corrected edition of the composer's solo sonatas; a note on the title page assured the public that 'This is more correct than the former edition'. Nevertheless, it includes two sonatas not actually by Handel, one of which – No. 12 in F, from which the above Allegro is taken – has become deservedly popular amongst violinists. All dynamics and slurs are editorial suggestions only. The Baroque technique used in bars 21 and 23, where a tune on one string is alternated with open string notes, is known as 'bariolage' and has the effect of creating maximum resonance.

© 2000 by The Associated Board of the Royal Schools of Music

Passamezzo

DO NOT PHOTOCOPY © MUSIC

Arranged by
Edward Huws Jones

ORTIZ

Diego Ortiz (*c.*1510–70) published his collection of music for solo viol, from which the above piece is taken, in 1553. The book is partly a tutor for learning to improvise above well-known chord sequences: this eight-bar sequence was called the 'passamezzo moderno'. In this arrangement, each repetition of the bass line supports a slightly different version of the melody. The whole piece needs to be played fast enough to be witty and flashy. EHJ

© Copyright 1996 by Faber Music Ltd

Reproduced from *The Young Violinist's Early Music Collection* by permission. All enquiries for this piece apart from the examinations should be addressed to Faber Music Ltd, 3 Queen Square, London WC1N 3AU.

DO NOT
PHOTOCOPY
© MUSIC

Country Dance

No. 4 from *Four Short Pieces*

BRIDGE

The *Four Short Pieces* were written in 1912, during the first part of Frank Bridge's (1879–1941) compositional career. It was not until the 1920s that Bridge moved away from the late-Romantic idiom apparent in the above piece to a more dissonant style, first seen in his Piano Sonata (1921–24).

© 1912 Stainer & Bell Ltd
Reproduced by permission. All enquiries for this piece apart from the examinations should be addressed to Stainer & Bell Ltd, PO Box 110, Victoria House, 23 Gruneisen Road, London N3 1DZ.

à Carice

Salut d'Amour

Op. 12

ELGAR

This beautiful piece – which translates as Love's Greeting – was completed in July 1888 just two months before Elgar's engagement to Caroline Alice Roberts, to whom it is dedicated.

© 1919 B. Schott's Söhne, Mainz
Reproduced by permission of Schott & Co. Ltd, London. All enquiries for this piece apart from the examinations should be addressed to Schott & Co. Ltd, 48 Great Marlborough Street, London W1V 2BN.

B:3

Stephanie–Gavotte

Op. 312

Adapted from an arrangement by
Johannes Palaschko

CZIBULKA

DO NOT
PHOTOCOPY
© MUSIC

This delightful piece needs to be played with a winning smile! One wonders what kind of person Stephanie might have been, and what she would think of 'her' piece being played for Grade 5. The section starting at bar 21 could give an opportunity for trying out spiccato.

© 1925 B. Schott's Söhne, Mainz
Reproduced by permission of Schott & Co. Ltd, London. All enquiries for this piece apart from the examinations should be addressed to Schott & Co. Ltd, 48 Great Marlborough Street, London W1V 2BN.

Oror

(Lullaby), Op. 1

ALAN HOVHANESS

DO NOT PHOTOCOPY © MUSIC

Edition Peters No. 6473. © 1964 by C. F. Peters Corporation, New York.
Reproduced by permission of Peters Edition Ltd, London. All enquiries for this piece apart from the examinations should be addressed to Peters Edition Ltd, 10–12 Baches Street, London N1 6DN.

Paragon Rag

C:2

DO NOT PHOTOCOPY © MUSIC

Arranged by
Edward Huws Jones

JOPLIN

Scott Joplin (1868–1917), the 'King of Ragtime', was an American composer and pianist who wrote numerous piano rags, and even a ragtime opera!

© Copyright 1994 by Boosey & Hawkes Music Publishers Ltd
Reproduced by permission. All enquiries for this piece apart from the examinations should be addressed to Boosey & Hawkes Music Publishers Ltd, 295 Regent Street, London W1B 2JH.

DO NOT
PHOTOCOPY
© MUSIC

Intermezzo

from *Háry János*

Arranged by
Peter Kolman

KODÁLY

Háry János, a singspiel by the Hungarian composer Zoltán Kodály (1882–1967), is the story of a veteran of the Napoleonic wars, boasting in the village inn of the adventures of his youth. In his fantastic account he describes how he rescued a lady in distress, single-handedly defeated Napoleon's army and won the heart of an Empress!

© 1927 by Universal Edition. This arrangement © 1988 by Universal Edition A. G., Wien.
Reproduced by permission. All enquiries for this piece apart from the examinations should be addressed to Universal Edition (London) Ltd,
48 Great Marlborough Street, London W1V 2BN.

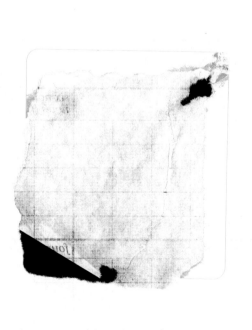

Checklist of Scales and Arpeggios

Candidates and teachers may find this checklist useful in learning the requirements of the grade. Full details of the forms of the various requirements, including details of rhythms, starting notes and bowing patterns, are given in the syllabus and in the scale books published by the Board.

Grade 5

			separate bows	slurred
Major Scales				*two beats to a bow*
	A♭ Major	2 Octaves		
	B Major	2 Octaves		
	C Major	2 Octaves		
	E♭ Major	2 Octaves		
	E Major	2 Octaves		
	G Major	3 Octaves		
Minor Scales (*melodic* or *harmonic*)				*two beats to a bow*
	G♯ Minor	2 Octaves		
	B Minor	2 Octaves		
	C Minor	2 Octaves		
	E Minor	2 Octaves		
	G Minor	3 Octaves		
Chromatic Scales				*four* or *six notes to a bow*
	on G	2 Octaves		
	on A	2 Octaves		
	on B♭	2 Octaves		
Major Arpeggios				*six notes (two-octave arpeggios) and three notes (three-octave arpeggio) to a bow*
	A♭ Major	2 Octaves		
	B Major	2 Octaves		
	C Major	2 Octaves		
	E♭ Major	2 Octaves		
	E Major	2 Octaves		
	G Major	3 Octaves		
Minor Arpeggios				*six notes (two-octave arpeggios) and three notes (three-octave arpeggio) to a bow*
	G♯ Minor	2 Octaves		
	B Minor	2 Octaves		
	C Minor	2 Octaves		
	E Minor	2 Octaves		
	G Minor	3 Octaves		
Dominant Sevenths				*...s to a bow*
	in B♭	1 Octave		
	in C	2 Octaves		
	in D	2 Octaves		
Diminished Sevenths				*four notes to a bow*
	on G	1 Octave		
	on D	1 Octave		
	on A	1 Octave		

GRADE
5

30129 037 319 788

NORFOLK LIBRARY AND
INFORMATION SERVICE

SUPP	CRAMER
INV.NO.	11411
ORD DATE	18.6.02

The Syllabus of Examinations should be read for details of requirements, especially those for scales, aural tests and sight-reading. Attention should be paid to the Special Notices on the inside front cover, where warning is given of any changes.

The syllabus is obtainable from music retailers or from The Associated Board of the Royal Schools of Music, 24 Portland Place, London W1B 1LU (please send a stamped addressed C5 (162mm × 229mm) envelope).

In examination centres outside the UK, information and syllabuses may be obtained from the Local Representative.

REQUIREMENTS

SCALES AND ARPEGGIOS (from memory)
in Ab, B, C, Eb, E majors; G#, B, C, E minors (two octaves) G major; G minor (three octaves)

Scales
in the above keys (minors in melodic *or* harmonic form at candidate's choice):
(i) separate bows
(ii) slurred, two beats to a bow

Chromatic Scales
starting on G, A and Bb (two octaves):
(i) separate bows, even notes
(ii) slurred, four *or* six notes to a bow at candidate's choice

Arpeggios
the common chords of the above keys:
(i) separate bows, even notes
(ii) slurred, six notes to a bow (two-octave arpeggios) and three notes to a bow (three-octave arpeggios)

Dominant Sevenths
in the keys of Bb (starting on F and resolving on the tonic) (one octave) and C and D (starting on G and A and resolving on the tonic) (two octaves):
(i) separate bows, even notes
(ii) slurred, four notes to a bow

Diminished Sevenths
starting on open strings G, D and A (one octave):
(i) separate bows, even notes
(ii) slurred, four notes to a bow

PLAYING AT SIGHT (see current syllabus)

AURAL TESTS (see current syllabus)

THREE PIECES   *page*

LIST A

LIST B

LIST C

Candidates must prepare three pieces, one from each of the three Lists, A, B and C. Candidates may choose from the pieces printed in this volume or any other piece listed for the grade. A full list is given in the current syllabus.

DO NOT
PHOTOCOPY
© MUSIC

© 2000 by The Associated Board of the Royal Schools of Music

No part of this publication may be copied or reproduced in any form or by any means without the prior permission of the publishers.

Music origination by Jack Thompson.

Cover by Økvik Design.

Printed in England by Halstan & Co. Ltd, Amersham, Bucks.

Where appropriate, pieces in this volume have been checked with original source material and edited as necessary for instructional purposes. Metronome marks, fingering, phrasing, bowing, and the editorial realization of ornaments (where given) are for guidance but are not comprehensive or obligatory.

Allegro con spirito

First movement from Sonata in D, Op. 16 No. 5

Edited by
Richard Jones

J. C. BACH

Johann Christian Bach (1735–82) was the famous Johann Sebastian's youngest son. This sonata is one of 33 written for piano or harpsichord 'with an accompaniment' for violin. Although the piano has the lion's share of the semiquavers, the violin holds its own in the musical conversation. Crossed slurs and bracketed dynamics and articulation marks (piano) are editorial suggestions only.

© 2000 by The Associated Board of the Royal Schools of Music

Allegro

Second movement from Sonata in F, Op. 1 No. 12, HWV 370

Edited by
Richard Jones

Attributed to HANDEL

In 1732 Handel's publisher John Walsh produced a corrected edition of the composer's solo sonatas; a note on the title page assured the public that 'This is more correct than the former edition'. Nevertheless, it includes two sonatas not actually by Handel, one of which – No. 12 in F, from which the above Allegro is taken – has become deservedly popular amongst violinists. All dynamics and slurs are editorial suggestions only. The Baroque technique used in bars 21 and 23, where a tune on one string is alternated with open string notes, is known as 'bariolage' and has the effect of creating maximum resonance.

© 2000 by The Associated Board of the Royal Schools of Music

A:3

Passamezzo

DO NOT PHOTOCOPY © MUSIC

Arranged by
Edward Huws Jones

ORTIZ

Diego Ortiz (*c.*1510–70) published his collection of music for solo viol, from which the above piece is taken, in 1553. The book is partly a tutor for learning to improvise above well-known chord sequences: this eight-bar sequence was called the 'passamezzo moderno'. In this arrangement, each repetition of the bass line supports a slightly different version of the melody. The whole piece needs to be played fast enough to be witty and flashy. EHJ

© Copyright 1996 by Faber Music Ltd

Reproduced from *The Young Violinist's Early Music Collection* by permission. All enquiries for this piece apart from the examinations should be addressed to Faber Music Ltd, 3 Queen Square, London WC1N 3AU.

DO NOT
PHOTOCOPY
© MUSIC

Country Dance

No. 4 from *Four Short Pieces*

BRIDGE

Allegretto moderato [♩. = *c*.63]

The *Four Short Pieces* were written in 1912, during the first part of Frank Bridge's (1879–1941) compositional career. It was not until the 1920s that Bridge moved away from the late-Romantic idiom apparent in the above piece to a more dissonant style, first seen in his Piano Sonata (1921–24).

© 1912 Stainer & Bell Ltd
Reproduced by permission. All enquiries for this piece apart from the examinations should be addressed to Stainer & Bell Ltd, PO Box 110, Victoria House, 23 Gruneisen Road, London N3 1DZ.

B:2

à Carice

Salut d'Amour

Op. 12

DO NOT PHOTOCOPY © MUSIC

ELGAR

This beautiful piece – which translates as Love's Greeting – was completed in July 1888 just two months before Elgar's engagement to Caroline Alice Roberts, to whom it is dedicated.

© 1919 B. Schott's Söhne, Mainz
Reproduced by permission of Schott & Co. Ltd, London. All enquiries for this piece apart from the examinations should be addressed to Schott & Co. Ltd, 48 Great Marlborough Street, London W1V 2BN.

B:3

Stephanie–Gavotte
Op. 312

Adapted from an arrangement by
Johannes Palaschko

CZIBULKA

DO NOT
PHOTOCOPY
© MUSIC

This delightful piece needs to be played with a winning smile! One wonders what kind of person Stephanie might have been, and what she would think of 'her' piece being played for Grade 5. The section starting at bar 21 could give an opportunity for trying out spiccato.

© 1925 B. Schott's Söhne, Mainz
Reproduced by permission of Schott & Co. Ltd, London. All enquiries for this piece apart from the examinations should be addressed to
Schott & Co. Ltd, 48 Great Marlborough Street, London W1V 2BN.

Oror

(Lullaby), Op. 1

ALAN HOVHANESS

DO NOT
PHOTOCOPY
© MUSIC

C:1

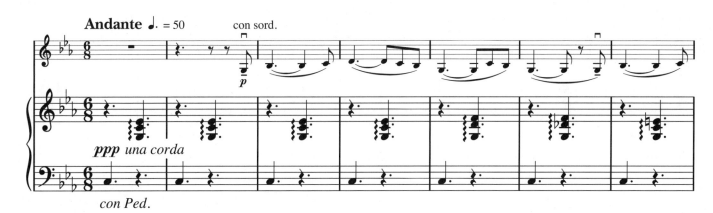

Edition Peters No. 6473. © 1964 by C. F. Peters Corporation, New York.
Reproduced by permission of Peters Edition Ltd, London. All enquiries for this piece apart from the examinations should be addressed to Peters Edition Ltd, 10–12 Baches Street, London N1 6DN.

con Ped.

C:2

Paragon Rag

DO NOT PHOTOCOPY © MUSIC

Arranged by
Edward Huws Jones

JOPLIN

Scott Joplin (1868–1917), the 'King of Ragtime', was an American composer and pianist who wrote numerous piano rags, and even a ragtime opera!

© Copyright 1994 by Boosey & Hawkes Music Publishers Ltd
Reproduced by permission. All enquiries for this piece apart from the examinations should be addressed to Boosey & Hawkes Music Publishers Ltd, 295 Regent Street, London W1B 2JH.

D. S. al Coda

CODA

DO NOT
PHOTOCOPY
© MUSIC

Intermezzo

from *Háry János*

Arranged by
Peter Kolman

KODÁLY

Andante maestoso, ma con fuoco [♩ = *c*.100]

Háry János, a singspiel by the Hungarian composer Zoltán Kodály (1882–1967), is the story of a veteran of the Napoleonic wars, boasting in the village inn of the adventures of his youth. In his fantastic account he describes how he rescued a lady in distress, single-handedly defeated Napoleon's army and won the heart of an Empress!

© 1927 by Universal Edition. This arrangement © 1988 by Universal Edition A. G., Wien.
Reproduced by permission. All enquiries for this piece apart from the examinations should be addressed to Universal Edition (London) Ltd, 48 Great Marlborough Street, London W1V 2BN.

Printed by
Halstan & Co. Ltd., Amersham, Bucks.